THE WORLD'S GREAT CLASSICAL MUSIC

Bach

47 Selections from Concertos, Chamber Works, Cantatas, and Keyboard Works

Cover Painting: Jan Steen, *Musical Company*, 1663

ISBN 978-0-634-03151-9

7777 W. BLUEMOUND RD. P.O. BOX 13819 MILWAUKEE, WI 53213

Visit Hal Leonard Online at
www.halleonard.com

CONTENTS

Pieces originally for keyboard; the remaining works are transcriptions for keyboard.

Table of ornaments and embellishments used in this book

ornament:

| Pralltriller | | mordent | turn | slide | slide and trill |

suggested execution:

ornament:

| turn and trill | appoggiaturas | appoggiatura and trill | long trill |

suggested execution:

etc.

The approximated rhythm and number of alternating notes in the trills will vary from case to case in Bach's music. This will depend largely on the tempo and lyric character of the piece, as well as the duration of the principal note. In the majority of cases, the Pralltriller should begin on the main note.

JOHANN SEBASTIAN BACH
(born March 21, 1685, Eisenach; died July 28, 1750, Leipzig)

Johann Sebastian Bach was the towering figure of Baroque music. Along with his contemporary George Frideric Handel, Bach forever defined the music of his era, creating a timeless body of remarkable music. Oddly enough, his genius as a composer was not widely recognized during his lifetime. It was not until 100 years later that audiences all over Europe began to hear Bach.

Born into a family with seven generations of musicians, Bach spent his early years in the German town of Eisenach, studying at the Latin School, where his cousin served as organist, making a profound impression on the young boy. By 1695, young Sebastian and brother Jacob were orphaned and sent to live with their older brother Johann Christoph in Ohrdruf. Bach studied organ with his brother and received a classical education for five years at the Lyceum school. He began to musically self-educate himself by hand copying his brother's scores. In 1700, when Christoph's home was becoming cramped, Sebastian headed for Lüneburg in northern Germany. His education continued while he sang in the choir until his voice broke, and then served as musician and organist. Sebastian's love for organ playing and organ building was nurtured here with directed musical studies and exposure to important organists from the north German school tradition. As a young man, Bach's curiosity and drive to hear and learn of various composers and performers outside of town often spurred him to make sojourns to other cities, managing this although nearly penniless. In 1703 he received his first official post as a musician at Arnstadt, where he played organ for services, and undoubtedly, composed music. He apparently walked thirty to sixty miles from Arnstadt to other cities to try to hear great organists of his day, including Dietrich Buxtehude. (Sebastian's inquiring musical mind and ambition to assimilate other composers' music, those past and also contemporaries like Vivaldi and Handel, were to pay lasting dividends in his own abilities as a composer.) The post at Arnstadt was not without tribulations, Sebastian's intolerance for less able musicians at the local church resulted in scuffles, and his exalted musical demands and long absences tried his employers.

Bach landed a better position as organist for the church of St. Blasius in Mühlhausen in 1707 where he started to compose cantatas and take pupils. Shortly thereafter, however, he and his pregnant wife, Maria Barbara, found themselves in Weimar. Sebastian was appointed as Duke Wilhelm's court organist and eventually Konzertmeister. He made his acquaintance with the famous Baroque composer Philipp Telemann, who even became godfather to one of the Bach sons, Emanuel. Sebastian composed six English keyboard suites, but his reputation as a harpsichordist, organist and supervisor for organ building also grew, his name first appearing in print by Johann Mattheson referring to him as the "famous Weimar organist." In 1717 he traveled to Dresden and was invited to compete at the harpsichord with the French virtuoso Louis Marchand, who apparently fled from the competition. Relations soured between Sebastian and the duke (Sebastian was even imprisoned for a short while) when Prince Leopold of Cöthen offered the composer a better paying position as Kapellmeister. The prince was a learned and true music lover who furnished Bach with living quarters, good musicians, and various instruments. Bach's stay at Cöthen (1717-1723) was a fertile period for his instrumental composition, which included the six Brandenburg concertos, six cello suites, two orchestral suites, *Clavier Büchlein* (Little Clavier Notebook), written for his eldest son, Wilhelm Friedemann, and the beginnings of his *Orgelbüchlein* (Little Organ Book) and *Das wohltemperirte Clavier* (The Well-Tempered Clavier). Bach's use of the word "clavier" referred generically to any keyboard instrument, most likely the harpsichord for a given occasion.

In July of 1720 Bach returned home from a trip with the prince to Carlsbad, only to discover that his wife had died and been already buried. In December of the following year he married Anna Magdalena, a singer who became an integral part of Bach's musical life as performer and copyist, and took to the task of raising a burgeoning family household. (It can be said that Bach's prolific output as a composer was proportionate to his prolific fathering of twenty children.) In 1722 the prestigious post as Kantor at the Thomaskirche in the commercial town of Leipzig became vacant, on account of the death of noted German composer Joseph Kuhnau, one of many regional composers whose music Bach studied. The vacancy at Leipzig brought in many strong candidates, including Telemann. However the list of applicants shrank because most were unable or unwilling to teach Latin as prerequisite. Bach was not the ecclesiastic council's first choice, but he was offered the position and settled in May of 1723, where he was to remain for the rest of his life. His responsibilities included director of music at Leipzig's four main churches, cantor at the St. Thomas school, and civic music director. He poured much of his energy into the composition of about 300 sacred cantatas for weekly services, an important part of the Lutheran liturgy. He had at his disposal many students and musicians under his direction to help fill the musical needs of the various churches in town.

Other important sacred works produced in Lepzig include the *St. Matthew Passion* (1727), the *Christmas Oratorio* (1734), several motets, and the monumental *Mass in B Minor* (1747). Bach continued to write instrumental music as well, including harpsichord concertos and a large collection of keyboard works published in installments entitled *Clavier Übung*. The collection included the six partitas, an Italian Concerto for keyboard, chorale preludes for organ, and the Goldberg Variations. The latter work was originally entitled "Aria with 30 variations" that Bach presented to Count von Keyserlingk in Dresden, who, by legend has it, had his harpsichordist, Johann Gottlieb Goldberg, play the variations to alleviate his insomnia. The variations are a virtuoso display of Bach's compositional technique in variation and canon. Bach was on continual demand as supervisor for new organs being built around the area, and he was consulted as well by the piano maker Gottfried Silbermann. By 1740, Sebastian taught less in the school and kept more private students. His most auspicious occasion may have been his visit to the court of Frederick the Great, King of Prussia, in Potsdam in 1747. There he gave concerts for the court, including a fugal improvisation on a theme supplied to him by the king. When returning home Bach worked diligently on *Musikalisches Opfer* (Musical Offering) which contained the improvised fugue plus several other movements for keyboard, flute and violin and continuo—all based on the king's theme. As Bach worked toward completing one of his last works, *Die Kunst der Fuge* (The Art of Fugue) he became blind, and his health weakened. He died at home leaving behind an estate stuffed with musical instruments and music manuscripts. Karl Phillip Emanuel saw to the completed publication of his father's *Art of Fugue*.

Bach staunchly believed in a thorough musical education for the Leipzig students and especially his own children. The family possessed many instruments, and many keyboard pieces were written specifically for one of Bach's sons. (Emanuel and brother Johann Christian would later become Sebastian's most successful heirs to the compositional craft.) Sebastian's creative impulses were often guided by a sense of pedagogical purpose. The forty-eight preludes and fugues, for instance, which comprise *The Well-Tempered Clavier* are an encyclopedic demonstration of all the various styles of Baroque fugue in all twenty-four keys of the chromatic scale. While Bach's fame did not become international until the mid-nineteenth century, study of this work became a regular staple of the musical diet for composers like Beethoven and Chopin. Bach fully embraced musical forms considered old fashioned in his time, but his exhaustive treatment and cultivation of the fugal device, his inventive rhythms and forward looking harmonic language paved the way and inspired the works of later composers. The last century has seen a great deal of scholarship on Bach, (including intriguing studies on mathematical properties of his music). His staggering number of works, unprecedented craftsmanship, and musical expression that attracts the senses and the intellect insures Bach's place in the performance world for generations to come.

Brandenburg Concerto No. 2 in F Major

First Movement Excerpt

Johann Sebastian Bach
1685-1750
BWV 1047
originally for orchestra

Air on The G String

from Orchestral Suite No. 3 in D Major

By Johann Sebastian Bach
1685-1750
BWV 1068
originally for orchestra

Brandenburg Concerto No. 3 in G Major
First Movement Excerpt

Johann Sebastian Bach
1685-1750
BWV 1048
originally for strings and continuo

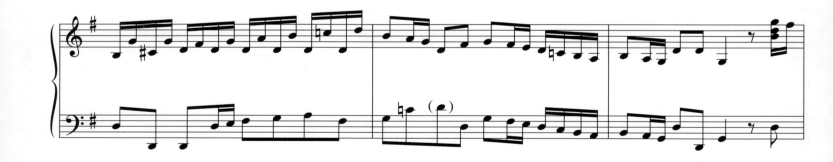

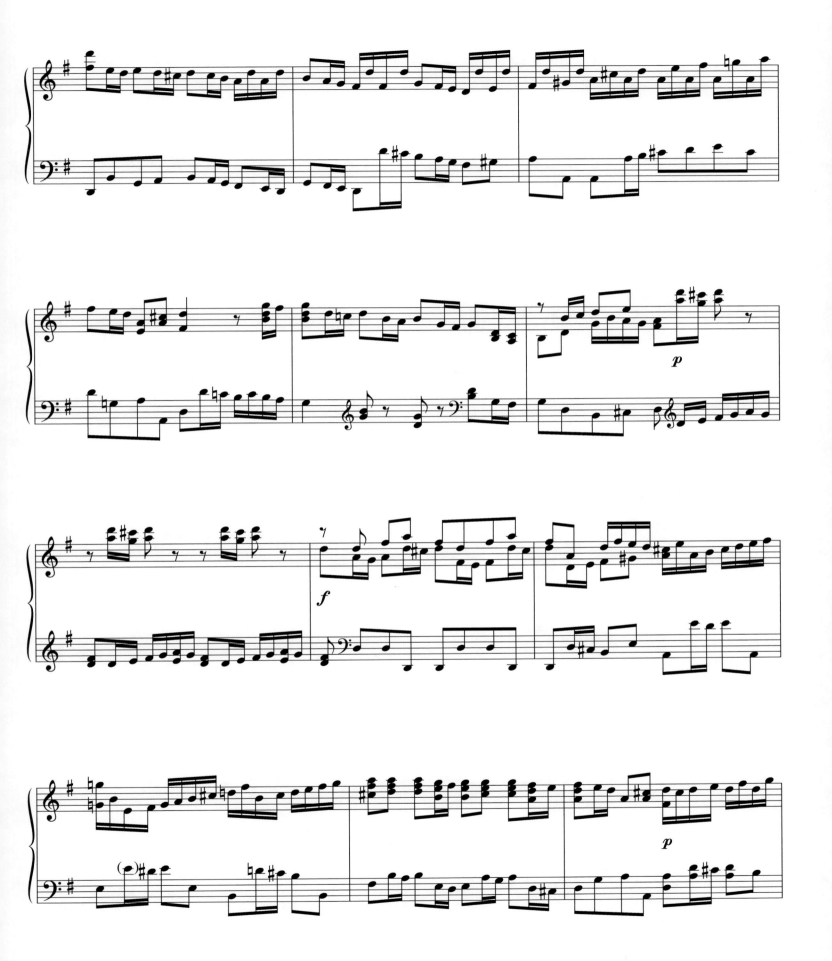

14

Brandenburg Concerto No. 4 in G Major

First Movement Excerpt

Johann Sebastian Bach
1685-1750
BWV 1049
originally for orchestra and continuo

Allegro

Brandenburg Concerto No. 5 in D Major

First Movement Excerpt

Johann Sebastian Bach
1685-1750
BWV 1050
originally for orchestra

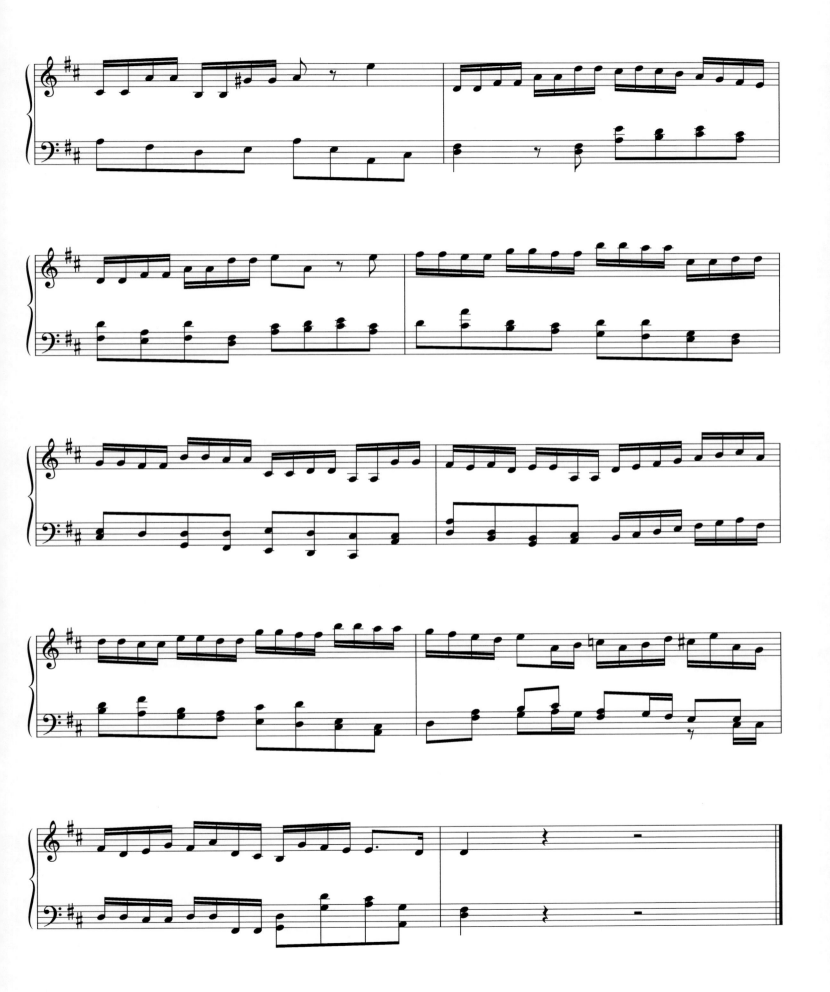

Brandenburg Concerto No. 6 in B-flat Major

Second Movement Excerpt

Johann Sebastian Bach
1685-1750
BWV 1051
originally for strings and continuo

Adagio ma non tanto

25

French Suite No. 2 in C Minor

Johann Sebastian Bach
1685-1750
BWV 813

Allemande
[Allegro moderato]

Courante
[Vivace]

31

Sarabande
[Andantino]

Air
[Andante]

1.

Menuet
[Allegretto]

Gigue
[Allegro]

Sarabande

from French Suite No. 3

Johann Sebastian Bach
1685–1750
BWV 814

Cello Suite No. 1 in G Major
Prelude

Johann Sebastian Bach
1685-1750
BWV 1007
originally for solo violoncello

[Andante]

Cello Suite No. 3 in C Major
Bourrée I

Johann Sebastian Bach
1685-1750
BWV 1009
originally for solo violoncello

[Andante]

Cello Suite No. 6 in D Major
Gavottes I and II

Johann Sebastian Bach
1685-1750
BWV 1012
originally for solo violoncello

GAVOTTE I
[Allegro moderato]

GAVOTTE II
[L'istesso Tempo]

English Suite No. 2 in A Minor

Johann Sebastian Bach
1685-1750
BWV 807

Prelude
[Allegro vivace]

Allemande
[Allegro moderato]

Courante
[Molto allegro]

Sarabande
[**Andante sostenuto**]

Bourrée I
[Molto allegro]

Bourrée II
[Moderato]

70

Bourrée I D.C.

Gigue
[Presto]

Gavotte
from French Suite No. 5

Johann Sebastian Bach
1685-1750
BWV 816

Jesu, joy of man's desiring

Jesus bleibet meine Freude
from Cantata No. 147, HERZ UND MUND UND TAT UND LEBEN

Johann Sebastian Bach
1685-1750
BWV 147
originally for choir and orchestra

Aria
from the GOLDBERG VARIATIONS

Johann Sebastian Bach
1685-1750
BWV 988

Jesus, priceless treasure
Chorale from Motet No. 3, JESU, MEINE FREUDE

Johann Sebastian Bach
1685-1750
BWV 227
originally for chorus

Little Prelude No. 2 in C Major

Johann Sebastian Bach
1685-1750
BWV 939

Keyboard Concerto No. 5 in F Minor
Second Movement, Largo (Arioso)

Johann Sebastian Bach
1685-1750
BWV 1056
originally for keyboard, strings and continuo

* This material was also adapted by Bach for his Cantata No. 156.

Little Prelude No. 3 in C Minor

Johann Sebastian Bach
1685-1750

[Allegro con moto]

87

Little Prelude No. 7 in E Minor

Johann Sebastian Bach
1685-1750
BWV 941

[Allegretto]

Little Prelude No. 8 in F Major

Johann Sebastian Bach
1685-1750
BWV 927

Quia respexit
from MAGNIFICAT

Johann Sebastian Bach
1685-1750
BWV 243
originally for soprano,
oboe d'amore and strings

Orchestral Suite No. 2 in B Minor
Badinerie and Menuet

Johann Sebastian Bach
1685-1750
BWV 1067
originally for flute, strings and continuo

BADINERIE
[Moderato]

MENUET
[L'istesso tempo]

Orchestral Suite No. 3 in D Major
Gavottes I and II

Johann Sebastian Bach
1685-1750
BWV 1068
originally for orchestra and continuo

GAVOTTE I
[Allegro]

GAVOTTE II

Partita No. 1 in B-flat Major

Johann Sebastian Bach
1685-1750
BWV 825

Prélude
[Moderato]

Allemande
[Allegro moderato]

Corrente
[Vivace]

Sarabande
[**Andante sostenuto**]

Menuet I
[Allegretto]

Menuet II
[Andante]

Gigue
[Allegretto con moto]

Partita No. 3 in E Major
Präludium (Prelude)

Johann Sebastian Bach
1685-1750
BWV 1006
originally for solo violin

[Allegro molto e con brio]

* This material was also adapted by Bach for lute.

125

Rest well, beloved
(Ruht wohl, ihr heiligen Gebeine)
from THE PASSION ACCORDING TO ST. JOHN

Johann Sebastian Bach
1685-1750
BWV 245
originally for chorus and orchestra

Passacaglia and Fugue in C minor
Excerpt

Johann Sebastian Bach
1685-1750
BWV 582
originally for organ

[Adagio]

131

Here bide we still with tears and weeping
(Wir setzen uns mit Tränen nieder)
from THE PASSION ACCORDING TO ST. MATTHEW

Johann Sebastian Bach
1685-1750
BWV 244
originally for chorus and orchestra

D.C. al Fine

Sheep may safely graze

from Cantata No. 208 ("Birthday Cantata")

Johann Sebastian Bach
1685-1750
BWV 208
originally for soprano,
2 flutes and continuo

Sleepers, awake
(Wachet auf, ruft uns die Stimme)
from Cantata No. 140

Johann Sebastian Bach
1685-1750
BWV 140
originally for tenor, strings and continuo

Siciliano
from SONATA NO. 2 FOR HARPSICHORD AND FLUTE

Johann Sebastian Bach
1685-1750
BWV 1031

146

Two-Part Invention No. 2 in C Minor

Johann Sebastian Bach
1685-1750
BWV 773

[Allegro moderato]

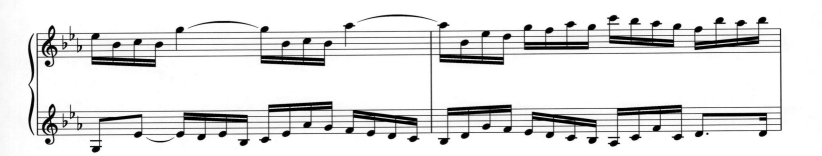

Two-Part Invention No. 1 in C Major

Johann Sebastian Bach
1685-1750
BMV 772

Two-Part Invention No. 7 in E Minor

Johann Sebastian Bach
1685-1750
BWV 778

Two-Part Invention No. 8 in F Major

Johann Sebastian Bach
1685-1750
BMV 779

[Vivace]

[mf]

Two-Part Invention No. 13 in A Minor

Johann Sebastian Bach
1685–1750
BWV 784

[Allegro tranquillo]

Two-Part Invention No. 14 in B-flat Major

Johann Sebastian Bach
1685–1750
BMV 785

[Andante con moto]

[f]

Two-Part Invention No. 15 in B Minor

Johann Sebastian Bach
1685-1750
BWV 786

Prelude and Fugue No. 1 in C Major

from THE WELL-TEMPERED CLAVIER, BOOK I

Johann Sebastian Bach
1685-1750
BWV 846

Prelude
[Allegro]

[*mp*]

Fugue (4 Voices)
[Andantino]

[mf]

[rit.]

Prelude and Fugue No. 2 in C Minor
from THE WELL-TEMPERED CLAVIER, BOOK I

Johann Sebastian Bach
1685-1750
BWV 871

Prelude
[Allegro]

Fugue (3 Voices)
[Allegretto]

Prelude and Fugue No. 5 in D Major

from THE WELL-TEMPERED CLAVIER, BOOK I

Johann Sebastian Bach
1685-1750
BWV 850

Prelude
[Allegro]

Fugue (4 Voices)
[Allegro maestoso]

[*f*]

Prelude and Fugue No. 6 in D Minor

from THE WELL-TEMPERED CLAVIER, BOOK I

Johann Sebastian Bach
1685-1750
BWV 851

Prelude
[Allegro]

[mf]

Fugue (3 Voices)
[Moderato]

Prelude and Fugue No. 11 in F Major
from THE WELL-TEMPERED CLAVIER, BOOK I

Johann Sebastian Bach
1685-1750
BWV 856

Prelude
[Allegro]

Fugue (3 Voices)
[Allegro]

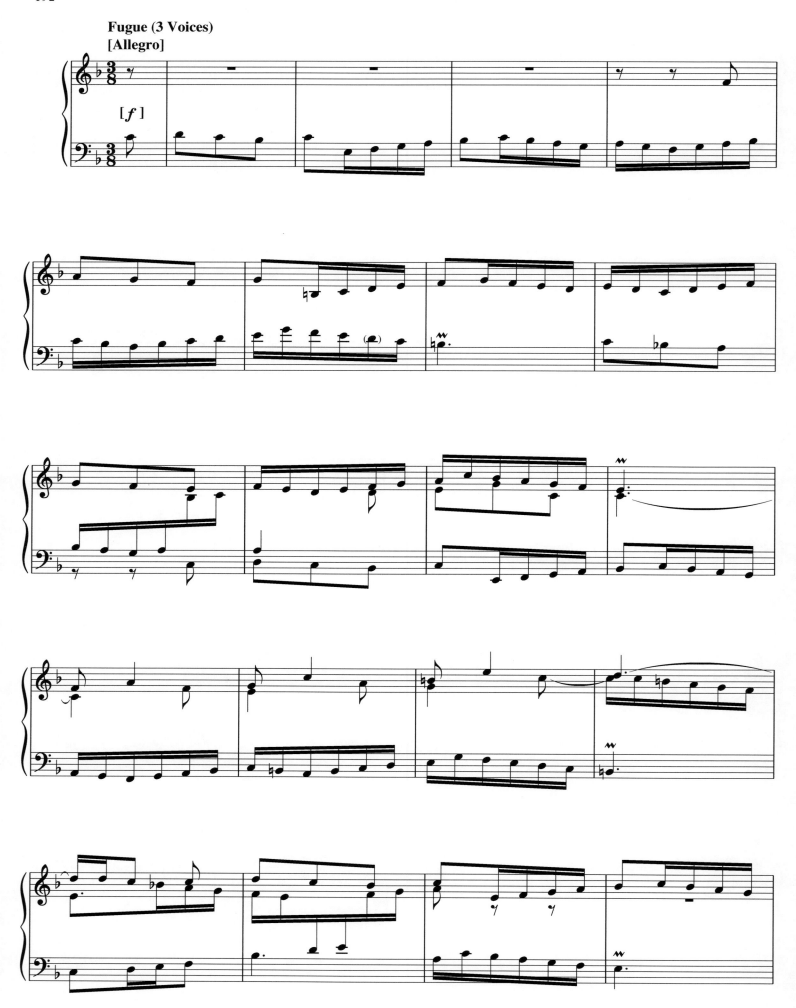

Prelude and Fugue No. 16 in G Minor

from THE WELL-TEMPERED CLAVIER, BOOK I

Johann Sebastian Bach
1685-1750
BWV 861

Prelude
[Andante]

197

Fugue (4 Voices)
[Moderato]

[*mf*]

Prelude and Fugue No. 21 in B-flat Major

from THE WELL-TEMPERED CLAVIER, BOOK I

Johann Sebastian Bach
1685–1750
BWV 866

Prelude
[Allegro]

[*f*]

Fugue (3 Voices)

[Allegro]

[*f*]